everyday
hope

everyday hope

---

365 WAYS TO A POSITIVE LIFE

An Hachette UK Company
www.hachette.co.uk

First published in 2019 by Pyramid,
an imprint of Octopus Publishing Group Ltd
Carmelite House
50 Victoria Embankment
London, EC4Y 0DZ
www.octopusbooks.co.uk

ISBN: 978-0-7537-3354-7

A CIP catalogue record for this book is
available from the British Library

Printed and bound in China

10 9 8 7 6 5 4 3 2 1

Publisher: Lucy Pessell
Designer: Lisa Layton
Design: Ummagumma
Editor: Sarah Vaughan
Contributing Editor: Emma Hill
Assistant Production Manager: Lucy Carter
Images: Shutterstock/Irtsya

INTRODUCTION

Hope (noun):

A feeling of expectation and desire for a particular thing to happen.

Grounds for believing that something good may happen.

"I hope that we have a good day at the fair."

In times of turmoil, how do we retain hope? How do we not allow cynicism and pessimism to become our natural mindset when the modern world seems to invite such an outlook on a daily basis? How can we nurture hope so that no matter what happens to, or around, us we have the resilience to smile and carry on? Behavioral research has shown that hope is not an emotion rather it's a way of thinking, a cognitive process. This means then that we can actually train ourselves to become more hopeful and to retain hope.

Everyday Hope brings you ideas on how to nurture hope daily, through goal setting, compassion, acceptance, self-improvement, connecting with others, gratitude, perseverance, self-care, celebration, and dwelling on the positive. Here you'll find a new exercise, tip, or inspirational quote for every day of the year to help you rise above difficulties with grace and ease, to live life with your light switched on.

Focus on nourishing hope and you will become more motivated to live your best year yet, regardless of circumstances. Use this book as your guide, inspiration, and motivation to find strength, joy, and faith in the future.

"Hope is the pillar that
holds up the world."

– PLINY THE ELDER

"If you are going through hell, keep going."

– WINSTON CHURCHILL

"Hope itself is like a star—
not to be seen in the sunshine
of prosperity, and only to
be discovered in the night
of adversity."

– CHARLES HADDON SPURGEON

CONSIDER THE EVIDENCE

Feel like there's no way you can make it through a particularly bleak day? Look back and consider the times when you've felt like this before. You're here now so your success rate in getting through tough times is 100%.

"Hope is the lone bloom
in the desert."

– TERRI GUILLEMETS

"Plant seeds of happiness, hope, success, and love; it will all come back to you in abundance. This is the law of nature."

– STEVE MARABOLI

CONNECT WITH OTHERS

Don't go it alone, connect to others who have been through similar battles to your own. Join a support group or online forum and find comfort and hope in the journeys of other people who truly understand what you're going through.

"Sometimes our light goes out, but is blown again into instant flame by an encounter with another human being."

– ALBERT SCHWEITZER

"Hope is the dream of a soul awake."

— FRENCH PROVERB

"Hope is an adventure, a going forward, a confident search for a rewarding life."

– DR. KARL MENNINGER

LEARN SOMETHING NEW

Learn a new language, enroll in an evening class, or take up a new hobby. The sense of achievement you'll gain through learning new skills will boost your confidence and make you hopeful that you can achieve anything you set your mind to.

"No matter where you are on your journey, that's exactly where you need to be. The next road is always ahead."

– OPRAH WINFREY

"What seems to us as bitter trials are often blessings in disguise."

– OSCAR WILDE

FIND SOLUTIONS

When obstacles block your path, try not to view them as insurmountable. Treat them as molehills not mountains and use your creativity and persistence to find solutions to overcome them.

"No matter what kind of difficult situation one may find oneself in, some opening, some opportunity to fight one's way out, can always be found. What's most important is to hold fast to Hope, to face the future with courage."

– DAISAKU IKEDA

"Hope is a light we keep inside that no one can touch."

– JERMAINE J. EVANS

REMIND YOURSELF THAT YOU ARE WORTHY

We're constantly bombarded by messages and advertising that tells us a myriad of ways we can improve ourselves—get thinner, richer, smarter...Remind yourself you're fine just the way you are. Repeat the mantra "I am worthy" on a daily basis.

"Kid, you'll move mountains!"

– DR. SEUSS

"It does not matter how slowly you go as long as you do not stop."

– CONFUCIUS

MOVE YOUR BODY

The mind–body link is unavoidable—it's impossible to have a healthy mind, to feel truly positive, if you're not looking after your body. So get moving! Exercise regularly to improve your fitness and increase endorphins and you'll feel more energized and hopeful.

"The very least you can do in your life is figure out what you hope for. And the most you can do is live inside that hope. Not admire it from a distance but live right in it, under its roof."

– BARBARA KINGSOLVER

"May your choices reflect your
hopes, not your fears."

– NELSON MANDELA

REMEMBER THAT YOU ARE THE CREATOR OF YOUR OWN WORLD

Imagine the world you want to live in, and create it…one small step at a time. You can fill it with acts of kindness and love; you can embrace optimism and shower affection on friends and family. Your environment becomes a reflection of all that you project on the world, so in this sense anything is possible.

"There is no medicine like hope, no incentive so great, and no tonic so powerful as expectation of something tomorrow."

– ORISON SWETT MARDEN

"Nature has fixed no limits on our hopes."

– BJÖRK

CREATE A DAILY MEDITATION RITUAL

Each day set aside some time to sit in silence and reflect, even just five minutes will bring its rewards. This nurturing act will help connect you to your soul and true purpose.

"Hope lights a candle instead of cursing the darkness."

– FATHER JAMES KELLER

CONSIDER ALL THE AMAZING THINGS YOU HAVE DONE

Look back and think about all of your life achievements. List these and let them serve as a reminder that you can do anything you set your mind to.

"Today's accomplishments
were yesterday's
impossibilities."

- ROBERT H. SCHULLER

"To hope is to
see with the eye
of the heart."

– SRI CHINMOY

BE COMPASSIONATE

By being generous and giving, you will gain a greater depth of understanding of your self and your own struggles. Plus you'll benefit from the feel-good factor of helping others.

"Hope is like the sun, which, as we journey toward it, casts the shadow of our burden behind us."

– SAMUEL SMILES

"You learn more from losing than winning. You learn how to keep going."

– MORGAN WOOTTEN

REACH OUT

Sharing your sufferings is a great way to gain support and perspective, so reach out to friends or family and tell them how you're feeling and what you're going through.

"You will face many defeats
in your life, but never let
yourself be defeated."

– MAYA ANGELOU

BE REALISTIC

Is the vision of the life you want to be leading, or the thing you want to happen, realistic? If not, make adjustments so that your vision is achievable and you therefore retain hope.

"Of all the forces that make for a better world, none is so indispensable, none so powerful, as hope. Without hope people are only half alive. With hope they dream and think and work."

– CHARLES SAWYER

DON'T DWELL ON WHAT YOU CAN'T CONTROL

It's all too easy for hope to dwindle if you focus on the aspects of any situation that you cannot control. Instead, concentrate on the things in life that you can control. For example, you can't control how your boss treats you, but you can control your reaction to that treatment, and you can make small steps to change the situation.

"Hope is a risk that
must be run."

– GEORGES BERNANOS

"All things are difficult
before they are easy."

– THOMAS FULLER

HAVE TRUST IN YOURSELF

Hope requires that you trust your ability to get through any situation. Consider writing some affirmations such as these to use when in need:

"I can do this."

"I will get through this."

"I am strong."

"Many of life's failures are people who did not realize how close they were to success when they gave up."

– THOMAS EDISON

NURTURE YOUR RELATIONSHIPS

In particular, nurture those relationships that are supportive and loving. Seek to spend time in the company of friends who encourage and empower you.

"Hope sees the invisible, feels the intangible, and achieves the impossible."

– HELEN KELLER

"Hope changes everything. It changes winter into summer, darkness into dawn, descent into ascent, barrenness into creativity, agony into joy."

– DAISAKU IKEDA

HAVE A SYMBOL OF HOPE

Designating an object as a symbol of hope is a great way to remind yourself there is life beyond whatever difficulties you are experiencing right now. Perhaps it's an inspirational painting, a feather, a gemstone, or a particular piece of jewelry. Whatever your chosen symbolic item, make sure it's positioned somewhere you will see it often, and when your eyes land on it let it be a reminder to remain hopeful.

"Even a single thread of hope is still a very powerful thing."

– LORRI FAYE

ACKNOWLEDGE YOUR STRENGTHS

Many of us don't have hope because we lack confidence. We feel we aren't worthy or don't have the ability to achieve certain goals. Counter this negative way of thinking by making a list of all your personal strengths. Refer to it whenever you need a confidence boost.

"Enthusiasm is the yeast that makes your hopes rise to the stars."

– HENRY FORD

"The best bridge between despair and hope is a good night's sleep."

– E. JOSEPH COSSMAN

GET THE BASICS RIGHT

Encourage a positive mindset by making healthy choices about the basics in life—food, sleep, exercise. Eat well, go to bed earlier, and move your body.

"What oxygen is to the lungs, such is hope to the meaning of life."

– EMIL BRUNNER

"Hope is always available to us. When we feel defeated, we need only take a deep breath and say, 'Yes,' and hope will reappear."

– MONROE FORESTER

ONE SMALL STEP...

When you feel so very far away from where you want to be, break down your journey into small steps. Can you do one thing that takes you a step closer to the place you want to be each day or week? Regularly ticking off incremental achievements will nurture hope.

"Hope is brightest when it dawns from fears."

– SIR WALTER SCOTT

"There are three things in life...not worrying what they are, not caring what others may think they are, and enjoying the wonder of what they might be."

– TOM ALTHOUSE

STEAL A MOMENT

Every day try to steal a moment for yourself to do something alone you enjoy—reading a book with a glass of wine, listening to your favorite music track, savoring the perfect mug of coffee in silence. Realize that whatever is going on in your life, you can gift yourself one happy moment of peace each and every day.

"Every moment has its pleasures
and its hope."

– JANE AUSTEN

"Hope never abandons you, you abandon it."

- GEORGE WEINBERG

"When you're at the end of your rope, tie a knot and hold on."

– THEODORE ROOSEVELT

STAY CALM

When things don't go perfectly to plan, resist getting emotionally riled up and try to stay calm. Stop and take a deep breath. Collect your thoughts and consider how you can move forward.

"While there's life,
there's hope."

– MARCUS TULLIUS CICERO

"When you have lost hope, you have lost everything. And when you think all is lost, when all is dire and bleak, there is always hope."

– PITTACUS LORE

DARE TO HAVE HOPE

Don't indulge in pessimistic thoughts. It's all too easy to caught up in a negative mindset that predicts an outcome of doom and gloom—in fact it's a comfort to do this, a way of having certainty in uncertain times. It's much braver to hope that all will be well.

"I steer my bark with hope in the head, leaving fear astern. My hopes indeed sometimes fail, but not oftener than the forebodings of the gloomy."

– THOMAS JEFFERSON

"Even your coldest winter,
Happens for better reasons,
And though it feels eternal,
Like all you'll ever do is freeze,
I promise spring is coming,
And with it brand new leaves."

– E.H

VISUALIZE YOUR PERFECT LIFE

Consider how you would like your ideal life to look—Where would you live? Who would you live with? What job what you do? What activities would you engage in? Who would be your friends?...Before you can have hope, you need to know what you are hoping for.

"Our imagination is the only limit to what we can hope to have in the future."

– CHARLES FRANKLIN KETTERING

"Don't lose hope.
Once the sun goes down,
the stars come out."

– UNKNOWN

"There was never a night or a problem that could defeat sunrise or hope."

– BERNARD WILLIAMS

LISTEN TO UPBEAT MUSIC

Music has the incredible ability to totally transform our mood. In times of adversity, use music to lift you out of low moods and feelings of hopelessness. Listen to upbeat, joyful tunes that have the power to instantly improve your outlook.

"If there is a reason to be hopeful, be hopeful. It doesn't jinx anything."

– UNKNOWN

"Sometimes the strength within you is not a fiery flame that all can see, it is just a tiny spark that whispers softly, 'You've got this, keep going.'"

– UNKNOWN

LOOK WITHIN

Hope is not something that just happens to you. You have to find it within, work on it, create it, and nurture it. Pause to reflect on how you can generate hope from your core being.

"To hope is to feel the presence of the inner sun. The inner sun is; the outer sun becomes."

– SRI CHINMOY

"If we will be quiet and
ready enough, we shall
find compensation in every
disappointment."

– HENRY DAVID THOREAU

REDUCE YOUR NEWS CONSUMPTION

We're constantly bombarded with news via our televisions, radios, and digital devices. Too much exposure can be detrimental to our emotional health and lead us into feelings of despair and hopelessness. Try to limit your news consumption to just one program, one newspaper, or 10 minutes of online news each day—enough to keep you in the loop but not so much that it damages your attitude.

"The world is indeed full of peril, and in it, there are many dark places; but still, there is much that is fair, and though in all lands love is now mingled with grief, it grows perhaps the greater."

– J.R.R. TOLKIEN

"Hope is a force of nature. Don't let anyone tell you different."

– JIM BUTCHER

DO SOMETHING FUN

Today build up your attitude of hopefulness by doing something you find fun. Go dancing, cook up a storm in the kitchen, go on a long bike ride…Anything that brings you pleasure will elevate your mood.

"Hope is the power
of being cheerful in
circumstances that we
know to be desperate."

– G.K. CHESTERTON

"Hope can be a powerful force. Maybe there's no actual magic in it, but when you know what you hope for most and hold it like a light within you, you can make things happen, almost like magic."

– LAINI TAYLOR

SWITCH UP YOUR THOUGHTS

Swap worry and regret for gratitude and appreciation. Each time you start to worry about something or dwell on past actions, actively bring your mind around to focus on something you are thankful for.

"There is nothing like a dream to create the future."

– VICTOR HUGO

"One of the best safeguards of our hopes, I have suggested, is to be able to mark off the areas of hopelessness and to acknowledge them, to face them directly, not with despair but with the creative intent of keeping them from polluting all the areas of possibility."

— WILLIAM F. LYNCH

AVOID PEOPLE WHO DRAIN YOU

In difficult times in particular it's very important not to be around people who consistently drain your energies. You need to conserve your emotional resources when times get tough, so make sure you are keeping good company.

"We can never give up longing and wishing while we are thoroughly alive. There are certain things we feel to be beautiful and good, and we must hunger after them."

– GEORGE ELIOT

HAVE A GAME PLAN

When you are facing a particular problem, write a step-by-step plan of attack. In doing this you will feel as though you are taking control of the situation and will become more hopeful of being able to overcome or deal with the issue at hand.

"Hold your head high, stick your chest out. You can make it. It gets dark sometimes, but morning comes. Keep hope alive."

– JESSE JACKSON

"However long
the night, the dawn
will break."

– AFRICAN PROVERB

"In the hopes of reaching the moon men fail to see the flowers that blossom at their feet."

– ALBERT SCHWEITZER

"Hope is the little voice you hear whisper 'maybe' when it seems the entire world is shouting 'no.'"

– UNKNOWN

SEIZE OPPORTUNITY

Go for that promotion, write a short story, take up a new sport, or start a college course…there is always an opportunity to be seized when you approach life with positivity and drive.

"Far away there in the sunshine are my highest aspirations. I may not reach them but I can look up and see their beauty, believe in them, and try to follow them."

– LOUISA MAY ALCOTT

"Do not spoil what you have
by desiring what you have not;
remember that what you now
have was once among the things
you only hoped for."

— EPICURUS

CULTIVATE AN ATTITUDE OF GRATITUDE

Being grateful for all that you have is the simplest way to encourage a hopeful outlook. Each night write down three things for which you are grateful and three good things that happened to you today, however small or insignificant they may seem.

"I don't think of all the misery, but of the beauty that still remains."

– ANNE FRANK

"Some see a hopeless end, while others see an endless hope."

– UNKNOWN

"Just don't give up
trying to do what you
really want to do.
When there is love and
inspiration, I don't think
you can go wrong."

– ELLA FITZGERALD

HAVE FAITH IN YOURSELF

Believe in your own ability to forge out a great future. Remember you have the power to make differences in your world.

"Keep your best wishes close to your heart and watch what happens."

— TONY DELISO

"Expect only the best from life and take action to get it."

– CATHERINE PULSIFER

MAKE PEACE WITH THE PAST

Don't get caught up going over old ground and dwelling on times when things didn't go to plan. Look instead at what you learned from that situation and make peace with it.

"It's amazing how a little tomorrow can make up for a whole lot of yesterday."

– JOHN GUARE

"Out of difficulties
grow miracles."

– JEAN DE LA BREYÈRE

CELEBRATE YOUR ALONE TIME

Make yourself a lovely dinner, open a bottle of bubbly, binge watch your favorite Netflix series, or run yourself a hot bath. This can serve as a great reminder to look to yourself for all that you need.

"Hope. It's like a drop of honey, a field of tulips blooming in the springtime. It's a fresh rain, a whispered promise, a cloudless sky, the perfect punctuation mark at the end of a sentence. And it's the only thing in the world keeping me afloat."

- TAHEREH MAFI

REMEMBER THAT YOUR LIFE IS MADE UP OF MANY PARTS

If one area in your life isn't going so well, focus on an area that is. Perhaps work is causing you stress, but you have a great relationship, or your relationship is crumbling but you have amazing friends. Focus on the positive.

"The greatest joys are found not only in what we do and feel, but also in what we hope for."

– BRYANT MCGILL

POSITIVE POSTURE

Make the most of the intrinsic mind–body connection and move your body from a place of positivity. Instantly improve your posture by standing or sitting up straight, un-hunching your shoulders, and holding your chin high. Notice the difference maintaining a powerful posture makes to the way you approach your day.

"Hope is being able to see that there is light despite all of the darkness."

– DESMOND TUTU

FIND A ROLE MODEL

Look at the attitudes and achievements of those around you.
Could any of them serve as a healthy role model for you?
If so, ask them for guidance and inspiration and let their
accomplishments inspire your own.

"People who build hope into their own lives and who share hope with others become powerful people."

– ZIG ZIGLAR

"Walk on with hope in
your heart, and you'll
never walk alone."

– SHAH RUKH KHAN

BUILD RESILIENCE

In order to remain hopeful even in times of turmoil, it's important to develop resilience. You need to learn how to function in distressing situations so consider practicing relaxation techniques, or call on friends who you consider part of your support system.

"Fear can hold you prisoner. Hope can set you free."

– STEPHEN KING

"The sky takes on shades of orange during sunrise and sunset, the color that gives you hope that the sun will set only to rise again."

– RAM CHARAN

"Hope is a song in a
weary throat."

– PAULI MURRAY

KEEP AN OPEN HEART

Hope can be found in the least expected places, so keep an open heart and an open mind.

"Hope is desire and expectation rolled into one."

– AMBROSE BIERCE

"Hope is man's preparation for
the unknown."

– SRI CHINMOY

"The only thing stronger than fear is hope."

– UNKNOWN

STEP OUT OF YOUR COMFORT ZONE

A great way to reset negative, hopeless thought patterns is to step out of your comfort zone. Shake up your life in small ways—wear bolder colors, say yes to the invitation that you'd normally turn down, step up on that podium to speak, try new foods, travel to a different country…

"If we remember those times and places where people have behaved magnificently, this gives us the energy to act."

– HOWARD ZINN

VISIT A HOMELESS SHELTER

Forget about your own troubles and cultivate positivity by helping out others who are less fortunate than you. Consider visiting a homeless shelter and handing out meals. Realize you have the power to change someone's day for the better.

"Each of us has the power to give life meaning, to make our time and our bodies and our words into instruments of love and hope."

– TOM HEAD

"Hope…is not a feeling; it is something you do."

– KATHERINE PATERSON

BE PROACTIVE

Hope is not passive. You need to actively invite it into your life and nurture it. Do this by taking positive actions to improve your situation at every turn.

"Most of the important things in the world have been accomplished by people who have kept on trying when there seemed to be no hope at all."

– DALE CARNEGIE

"Hope is the 'yes'
to life."

– DR. RONNA JEVNE

SCRUTINIZE YOUR DOUBTS

We all have moments when we doubt our abilities, we doubt that we can put things right, or alter our direction of travel. Doubts often get sown very early in life and don't stand up to later scrutiny. So put your doubts into words. Chances are as you review them, many of them won't actually make much sense and you can simply discard them.

"Nothing is permanent in this wicked world, not even our troubles."

– CHARLIE CHAPLIN

"Though one door is shut,
there are thousands still
open to you."

— RUCKETT

"No matter how far down you go, it is never too late to come back."

– THEO FLEURY

FIND THE LESSON

Being hopeful means treating the challenges that you face in a positive way. Instead of letting your difficulties overwhelm you, look instead for the lesson each obstacle you're confronted with is teaching you. There is always some wisdom to be gained in tricky times.

"Only in the darkness can you see the stars."

– MARTIN LUTHER KING, JR.

"Character consists of what
you do on the third and
fourth tries."

– JAMES A. MICHENER

LEARN TO LAUGH AT YOURSELF

Even when you feel as though you're failing, find a way to take a step back and laugh at yourself.

"I have seen what a laugh can do. It can transform almost unbearable tears into something bearable, even hopeful."

– BOB HOPE

BRING FRESH ENERGY INTO YOUR HOME

Repaint the walls, scatter plants throughout your living space, rearrange furniture, buy a new painting, string up some fairy lights…However small the gesture, making changes to your home environment can help alleviate feelings of being stuck in a rut and will usher in a more hopeful energy.

"Where there is no vision,
there is no hope."

– GEORGE WASHINGTON CARVER

"You are full of unshaped dreams...
You are laden with beginnings...
There is hope in you..."

– LOLA RIDGE

DWELL ON THE POSITIVE

In order to magnify feelings of positivity think back on moments in your life when you have felt pure joy or happiness.

"Hope is definitely not the same thing as optimism. It is not the conviction that something will turn out well, but the certainty that something makes sense, regardless of how it turns out."

– VÁCLAV HAVEL

THERE IS ALWAYS SOMETHING YOU CAN DO

No matter what it is that's bothering you, remind yourself there's always something you can do about it. Sit down and write a plan of action.

"The person who says it cannot be done should not interrupt the person who is doing it."

– CHINESE PROVERB

"Hope begins in the dark, the stubborn hope that if you just show up and try to do the right thing, the dawn will come."

– ANNE LAMOTT

RESPOND WITH LOVE

If another person is being rude and taking their bad mood out on you, try to respond with kindness and patience. Let their insults effortlessly roll off you and appreciate that the person doing you wrong is likely facing their own struggles. Don't let them drag you into their realm of negativity.

"Hope rejects cynicism and bitterness as unhelpful, and is perennially proved right."

– DOUG MUDER

"Hope is a walk through a flowering meadow. One does not require that it lead anywhere."

– ROBERT BRAULT

"But groundless hope,
like unconditional love,
is the only kind worth
having."

– JOHN PERRY BARLOW

"This is where it all begins. Everything starts here, today."

– DAVID NICHOLLS

BREAK BAD HABITS

When put in difficult situations we tend to react in the same way each time—we are hardwired to respond to situations in the same manner over and over again. Consciously break these behavior patterns and start afresh.

"Hope means believing in spite of the evidence, and then watching the evidence change."

– JIM WALLIS

"We must accept finite disappointment, but never lose infinite hope."

– MARTIN LUTHER KING, JR.

TAKE LIFE AS IT COMES

Accept situations and life events as they are and work with them. Living in denial or burying your head in the sand blocks hope.

"Trust the wait. Embrace the uncertainty. Enjoy the beauty of becoming. When nothing is certain, anything is possible."

– UNKNOWN

"Man needs, for his happiness, not only the enjoyment of this or that, but hope and enterprise and change."

– BERTRAND RUSSELL

"Hope is itself a species of happiness and, perhaps, the chief happiness which this world affords."

– SAMUEL JOHNSON

MAKE HAPPINESS YOUR GOAL

Happiness and hope go hand in hand. Create some happiness affirmations like the examples below and repeat them to yourself on a daily basis:

"Happiness flows through me like a river to the sea."

"I breathe deeply and I am happy."

"Happiness is my natural state of being."

"If winter comes, can spring be far behind?"

– PERCY BYSSHE SHELLEY

HAVE A SENSE OF PURPOSE

Set long-term goals that you can slowly but surely move toward.
Include one achievable item on your to-do list every single day
that works toward attaining this goal.

"If you want to build a ship, don't herd people together to collect wood and don't assign them tasks and work, but rather teach them to long for the endless immensity of the sea."

– ANTOINE DE SAINT-EXUPÉRY

"Hopeful, we are halfway to where we want to go; hopeless, we are lost forever."

– LAOZI

RETREAT

Retreat to your center in times of need to find encouragement and strength. How do you find your center? Ask yourself what you love in this world more than yourself, more than life itself. That's where your core being lies.

"We dream to give ourselves hope. To stop dreaming—well, that's like saying you can never change your fate."

– AMY TAN

PRIORITIZE SELF-CARE

It's impossible to develop a hopeful attitude if you don't take good care of yourself. Set time aside each day to fill your cup, whether you go on a brisk walk, practice yoga, go to a gym class, meditate, or simply curl up with a good book.

"I dwell in possibility."

– EMILY DICKINSON

"Sanity may be madness but the maddest of all is to see life as it is and not as it should be."

– DON QUIXOTE

"Fear grows in darkness;
if you think there's a
bogeyman around, turn
on the light."

– DOROTHY THOMPSON

SMILE

Trick your mind into feeling more hopeful simply through curling up the corners of your mouth.

"Hope smiles from the threshold of the year to come, whispering 'it will be happier...'"

– ALFRED TENNYSON

LOOK UP

Throw your head back and look at the sky. Breathe deeply and take a moment to reflect on the world as a whole, and all the other people under this vast sky. Doing this can really help you to gain perspective.

"If you have a heartbeat, there's still time for your dreams."

– SEAN STEPHENSON

"Where some see despair, others see hope. Hope then, like beauty, is in the eye of the beholder."

– WENDY EDEY

WORK ON YOUR ATTITUDE

Accept that hope is not a constant state of mind and that each day you need to work toward cultivating a hopeful attitude.

"Things start out as hopes
and end up as habits."

– LILLIAN HELLMAN

"Hope is the only
bee that makes honey
without flowers."

– ROBERT G. INGERSOLL

SPEND TIME WITH PEOPLE WHO INSPIRE OPTIMISM

There's nothing that raises your levels of hopefulness quite like spending time around hopeful, optimistic people. Just like despair, optimism is contagious.

"Optimism is the faith
that leads to achievement.
Nothing can be done without
hope and confidence."

– HELEN KELLER

"The hopeful man sees
success where others
see failure, sunshine
where others see
shadows and storm."

— ORISON SWETT MARDEN

"One of the finest lessons nature can teach us is that of hope. She shows us hope realized with every bud that blossoms and every bird that learns to fly."

– UNKNOWN

TAKE UP GARDENING

There are so many hopeful sights to be found in a garden—new shoots sprouting where you planted seeds, buds opening on flowers you have tended, trees bearing fruit…If you don't have a garden, plant window boxes and watch them bloom.

"All it takes is one bloom of hope to make a spiritual garden."

– TERRI GUILLEMETS

"The road that is built in hope is more pleasant to the traveler than the road built in despair, even though they both lead to the same destination."

– MARION ZIMMER BRADLEY

"Where there is a
ruin, there is hope
for treasure."

– RUMI

BELIEVE IN HUMANITY

Remember that however dark and depressing a place the world can seem, the light of humanity shines through it all. Read stories of people who have made the world a brighter place in their darkest hours to counterbalance the bad news that gets fed to us daily.

"Look at how a single candle can both defy and define the darkness."

– ANNE FRANK

"Fairy tales are more than true: not because they tell us that dragons exist, but because they tell us that dragons can be beaten."

– NEIL GAIMAN

KEEP GOING

When the future is clouded with uncertainty and your path becomes rocky, just keep moving forward. Forge ahead and know that with each step you are getting closer to brighter times.

"Before you give up, think of the reason why you held on so long."

– UNKNOWN

"Hold fast to dreams,
For if dreams die
Life is a broken-winged bird,
That cannot fly."

– LANGSTON HUGHES

VISUALIZE YOUR BEST SELF

Visualize your best possible self a year from now. Consider how to use your abilities and strengths to realize this vision.

"A strong mind always hopes, and has always cause to hope."

– THOMAS CARLYLE

"Never let go of hope—
dream, take action, and
get that transfer to live the
life you wish."

– CATHERINE PULSIFER

BE NICE

Thank store assistants, smile at strangers in the street, say a friendly hello to passing acquaintances…As this becomes your norm, you'll notice that these niceties get returned to you, naturally raising your feelings of hope and optimism.

"Hope is the feeling you have that the feeling you have isn't permanent."

– JEAN KERR

"In our lives, where there is hope, the impossible moves within our grasp, and what seems difficult to reach waits but a breath away."

– UNKNOWN

TAKE THE EASY WAY

Are there any shortcuts you can take when it comes to achieving your goal or overcoming obstacles? Often we put so much pressure on ourselves and think the "right" path to choose is the most difficult one. Instead, consider how you can make your journey easier.

"There is always hope for a new day, hope that the darkness won't always seem impenetrable."

– MARCIA LAYCOCK

"Where there is no hope, it is incumbent on us to invent it."

– ALBERT CAMUS

CELEBRATE SMALL VICTORIES

Before you go to bed, mentally review your day and celebrate all the steps you took to achieve your goal or overcome your obstacle. Perhaps you went to the gym—one step toward your fitness goal, or you finally called a friend to open up about something that has been bothering you.

"Hope does not leave
without being given
permission."

– RICK RIORDAN

"Hope doesn't come from calculating whether the good news is winning out over the bad. It's simply a choice to take action."

– ANNA LAPPÉ

QUESTION YOUR STORY

Write down your worries and then remove any hyperbole. Are things really that bad? What stories are you telling yourself? Are you exaggerating certain aspects? This is a great way to get really honest with yourself and will often lead to the elimination of unnecessary fretting.

"The difference between hope and despair is a different way of telling stories from the same facts."

– ALAIN DE BOTTON

DO WHAT YOU LOVE

Engage in activities that you feel a passion for. Whatever it is, if you love doing it, positive feelings and therefore hope will be ignited.

"We always kept in our hearts the most noble, beautiful feeling that sets human beings apart: hope."

– MANEL LOUREIRO

"Hope is a renewable option: If you run out of it at the end of the day, you get to start over in the morning."

– BARBARA KINGSOLVER

ENGAGE IN POSITIVE SELF-TALK

There are several cognitive strategies that can help restore and nurture hope. One is through practicing positive self-talk. Every time you find yourself thinking you can't do something, check yourself and instead find reasons why you can. Re-frame any negative thoughts you have about your personality or abilities in a positive light.

"Think big and don't listen to people who tell you it can't be done. Life's too short to think small."

– TIM FERRISS

"Strong hope is a much greater stimulant to life than any single realized joy could be."

– FRIEDRICH NIETZSCHE

"To live without hope is to cease to live."

– FYODOR DOSTOYEVSKY

"I am prepared for the worst, but hope for the best."

– BENJAMIN DISRAELI

"Hope is like a road in the country; there was never a road, but when many people walk on it, the road comes into existence."

– LIN YUTANG

SEND MESSAGES OF GRATITUDE

Invite positivity into your life by sending text messages, emails, or letters of appreciation to friends and family—just a line to tell them how much you appreciate them and why. In turn, their responses will show you how much they care, too.

"Hope is the best possession."

— WILLIAM HAZLITT

"If we expect change we must act on our hope every day until we have accomplished what we wanted."

– CHRISTOPHER GOODMAN

FIND A CAUSE

Get involved in a cause and volunteer your time and skills to help fundraise or organize charitable events. This is a great way to help cultivate hope for the future and future generations.

"Each time a person stands up for an ideal, or acts to improve the lot of others, or strikes out against injustice, he sends forth a tiny ripple of hope."

– ROBERT F. KENNEDY

LIST YOUR SUCCESSES

Look back at times in the past when you have successfully overcome difficulties. List the ways in which you did this and use this past success to foster hope that you can and will overcome future obstacles.

"Never lose hope. Storms make people stronger and never last forever."

– ROY T. BENNETT

"Hope is important because it can make the present moment less difficult to bear. If we believe that tomorrow will be better, we can bear a hardship today."

– THICH NHAT HANH

FRAME HOPE IN A POSITIVE WAY

Use positive language when contemplating your hopes. Focus on what you DO want as opposed to what you DON'T want.

"If it were not for hope, the
heart would break."

– THOMAS FULLER

"It is hope that gives life meaning. And hope is based on the prospect of being able one day to turn the actual world into a possible one that looks better."

– FRANÇOIS JACOB

LOOK FORWARD TO THE DAY AHEAD

If you catch yourself making gloomy predictions for the day ahead, instead switch your focus onto all the positive things you have to look forward to today. These don't have to be huge events, but simple everyday pleasures such as a good cup of coffee, a new episode of your favorite television show, or a delicious dinner.

"Practice hope. As hopefulness becomes a habit, you can achieve a permanently happy spirit."

– NORMAN VINCENT PEALE

"The capacity for hope is the most significant fact of life. It provides human beings with a sense of destination and the energy to get started."

– NORMAN COUSINS

MAKE STEPS TO IMPROVE YOUR LIFE

Your health is an important place to begin—make any necessary changes to your diet and lifestyle to give yourself every hope of remaining healthy or restoring optimum health.

"Hope is that thing inside us that insists, despite all the evidence to the contrary, that something better awaits us if we have the courage to reach for it and to work for it and to fight for it."

– BARACK OBAMA

EXPAND YOUR HORIZON

The best way to do this is through spiritual practice, which will help you to get out of your head and recognize that the horizon lies way beyond whatever is happening in your life right now. Perhaps you engage in spirituality through yoga, a mindfulness meditation, or a walk in nature…whichever speaks to you will help you to gain perspective from a higher viewpoint.

"Hope is the companion of power, and mother of success; for who so hopes strongly has within him the gift of miracles."

– SAMUEL SMILES

"Men and women are limited not by the place of their birth, not by the color of their skin, but by the size of their hope."

– JOHN JOHNSON

REMEMBER EVERYTHING IS POSSIBLE

To have a better day tomorrow, to find love, to change career…
However ambitious your hopes, remember nothing
is impossible.

"Once you choose hope, anything's possible."

– CHRISTOPHER REEVE

"I have learned to use the word 'impossible' with the greatest caution."

– WERNHER VON BRAUN

FIND MEANING

If you feel your life has meaning it is much easier to live with hope in your heart. So how do you find your life's true purpose? One trick is to ask yourself what you would do with your life if you only had one year to live. Your answer will clarify what you truly value and therefore what you should be prioritizing.

"Hope is medicine for a soul that's sick and tired."

– ERIC SWENSSON

"Hope is a vigorous principle...it sets the head and heart to work, and animates a man to do his utmost."

– JEREMY COLLIER

STRENGTHEN YOUR RELATIONSHIPS

Make a special effort with your partner—cook them their favorite meal, plan a surprise trip for them, or simply pay them a compliment. Take the time to call your friends or meet up face-to-face instead of just texting them. Visit family members you haven't seen in while. Weave positivity and warmth through all these precious relationships.

"I know the world is filled with troubles and many injustices. But reality is as beautiful as it is ugly. I think it is just as important to sing about beautiful mornings as it is to talk about slums. I just couldn't write anything without hope in it."

– OSCAR HAMMERSTEIN II

"Hope is a choice of courage."

- TERRI GUILLEMETS

"Remember. Hope is a good thing, maybe the best of things, and no good thing ever dies."

– STEPHEN KING

"There are far, far better things ahead than anything we leave behind."

– C.S. LEWIS

"None of us knows what might happen even the next minute, yet still we go forward. Because we trust. Because we have Faith."

– PAULO COELHO

CELEBRATE ACCOMPLISHMENTS

Plan ways to celebrate your achievements with friends and family—throw a party, go out for dinner...Don't let all your small victories simply float by unnoticed and unacknowledged.

"In all things it is better to hope than to despair."

– JOHANN WOLFGANG VON GOETHE

"In time of trouble avert not thy face from hope, for the soft marrow abideth in the hard bone."

– HAFEZ

"Hope is only the love
of life."

– HENRI FRÉDÉRIC AMIEL

"It's the possibility that keeps me going, not the guarantee."

– NICHOLAS SPARKS

SET PERSONAL GOALS

Make sure the goals you set aren't based on external factors over which you have no control. For example, you may be aiming to win a competition or a race, but you have no control over the judges' decision or the other competitors, so you're relying on the actions of other people. Instead, make the goal a personal one (a personal best running time, for example), or set goals reliant on yourself such as learning a new skill—anything where the outcome is dependent solely on you and your actions.

"If we can get to the place where we show up as our genuine selves and let each other see who we really are, the awe-inspiring ripple effect will change the world."

– TERRIE M. WILLIAMS

"In the midst of winter,
I found there was, within
me, an invincible summer."

– ALBERT CAMUS

MAKE YOUR VOICE HEARD

Go on a mass march, take part in peaceful protests, write letters to express concerns, start local initiatives…Whatever it is you feel strongly about, make an effort to get your voice heard and you'll feel more hopeful about the future, knowing that you're playing some small part in helping to make things better.

"I have not the shadow of a doubt that any man or woman can achieve what I have, if he or she would make the same effort and cultivate the same hope and faith."

– MAHATMA GANDHI

"My great hope is to laugh as much as I cry; to get my work done and try to love somebody and have the courage to accept the love in return."

– MAYA ANGELOU

EXPRESS YOUR LOVE

Hug your partner, kiss your children often, tell friends you love them...Expressing your love on a daily basis will help to bring meaning, warmth, and positivity into your life.

"In all pleasures hope is a considerable part."

– SAMUEL JOHNSON

"Thoughts lead to words, words lead to actions, and hope is the thread that binds up each."

– AIMEE ANGLE

TAKE RISKS

Make shifts in your lifestyle when needed to avoid feeling stuck.
This way life keeps moving forward.

"Our greatest glory is not in never falling, but in rising every time we fall."

– CONFUCIUS

"Hope is faith holding out its hand in the dark."

– GEORGE ILES

SEEK INSPIRATION

Read real-life stories of people who have achieved your ambition or made it through similar troubles to your own. Find case studies online or read inspirational biographies and let others' successes ignite your hope.

"You find hope the same way you find happiness. You give it to someone else and borrow a little of it back."

– ROBERT BRAULT

FIND YOUR STRENGTH

It's often in adversity that we come to realize our inner strength.
Challenges in life will help you to develop characteristics
you never knew you had, to connect to your inner core, and
to therefore move forward with greater self-knowledge and
renewed hope.

"We need never be hopeless because we can never be irreparably broken."

– JOHN GREEN

"For yesterday is but a dream,
And to-morrow is only a vision;
But to-day well lived makes
Every yesterday a dream of happiness,
And every tomorrow a vision of hope."

– KĀLIDĀSA

LIVE IN THE MOMENT

Although it's important to visualize a bright future in order to foster hope, it's making the most of the present moment that gives you the best chance of making that future a reality.

"The present is the ever moving shadow that divides yesterday from tomorrow. In that lies hope."

– FRANK LLOYD WRIGHT

NEVER COMPARE

Comparing yourself to other people is a futile exercise that frequently leads to dissatisfaction and feelings of hopelessness. Make it a life rule to never compare yourself to other people. You have no idea what journey they are on or what internal challenges they are facing; stick to your own path.

"Nobody trips over mountains. It is the small pebble that causes you to stumble. Pass all the pebbles in your path and you will find you have crossed the mountain."

– UNKNOWN

USE YOUR INTUITION

Listen to the voice that comes from deep within and let it guide you.

"Hang on to your hat.
Hang on to your hope.
And wind the clock, for
tomorrow is another day."

– E.B. WHITE

"As I see it, in everything that we do, we need to come down on the side of life and hope."

– F. TUSTIN

APPRECIATE THE SMALL THINGS

Look around you and try to appreciate all the small, beautiful things that often go unnoticed, whether it be an act of kindness, a beautiful flower, the laughter of a child, the smile of a loved one…remembering that each is a precious gift will help you maintain a positive mindset.

"This new day is too dear, with its hopes and invitations, to waste a moment on the yesterdays."

– RALPH WALDO EMERSON

"As long as we have hope, we have direction, the energy to move, and the map to move by."

– LAOZI

FOCUS ON WHAT YOU CAN DO FOR OTHERS

How can you use your own experiences and journey to help others? Maybe you are going through tough times, but by sharing your experience and the knowledge you are gaining you could help others who are going through similar struggles. Share your stories on a forum, or consider writing a blog. Seeing you are helping others will increase your own feelings of well-being and give you a renewed sense of purpose.

"You must not lose faith in humanity. Humanity is an ocean; if a few drops of the ocean are dirty, the ocean does not become dirty."

– MAHATMA GANDHI

"Every area of trouble gives out a ray of hope: and the one unchangeable certainty is that nothing is certain or unchangeable."

– JOHN F. KENNEDY

BE FLEXIBLE

Learn to adapt to changing situations. If you can alter your approach, modify the way you tackle your challenges, and reach for your goals when necessary, you have a far greater chance of remaining hopeful.

"When you get into a tight place and everything goes against you, till it seems as though you could not hang on a minute longer, never give up then, for that is just the place and time that the tide will turn."

– HARRIET BEECHER STOWE

IMAGINE YOURSELF HOPEFUL

Use possibility thinking and picture yourself waking up each day full of hope. Visualize your day going well and then step into it with a positive attitude.

"Everything you can imagine is real."

– PABLO PICASSO

"Hope is but the dream
of those who wake."

– MATTHEW PRIOR

HELP SOMEONE IN NEED

Reach out to a neighbor who may need help or just company, or a friend in turmoil, or volunteer for a local charity. Each compassionate act, however small, helps to bring a little more peace and hope to the world.

"I am not an optimist, because I am not sure that everything ends well. Nor am I a pessimist, because I am not sure that everything ends badly. I just carry hope in my heart."

– VÁCLAV HAVE

"A life without hope is bleak and grey. If you have no hope, create some."

– DAISAKU IKEDA

INDULGE IN HAPPY MEMORIES

When life gets tough, go through photographs of happy times and indulge in the memories. Let them serve as a reminder that life was once good so there is every hope that it will be again.

"Hope is patience with the lamp lit."

– TERTULLIAN

"Hope is not a matter of waiting for things outside of us to get better. It is about getting better inside about what is going on outside."

— JOAN CHITTISTER

PRACTICE MINDFULNESS

Grounding yourself in the present moment will help you to stop agonizing over things that have already happened and worrying about what is to come. Try the following exercise:

1. Select a natural object—maybe a leaf, a sea shell, or a crystal—in your immediate environment and focus on it for a few minutes.

2. Do nothing other than notice this object for as long as your concentration allows.

3. Look at this object as if you are seeing it for the very first time.

4. Visually explore every aspect of its appearance and try to become totally consumed by its presence.

5. Relax and allow yourself to connect to its energy and purpose within the natural world.

"Hope is the thing with feathers, that perches in the soul, and sings the tune without the words and never stops at all."

– EMILY DICKINSON

"In joined hands there is still some token of hope, in the clinched fist none."

– VICTOR HUGO

LOOK FOR THE BEST IN PEOPLE

If you find someone disagreeable, seek out a good trait they have. Do the same with everyone you meet. If you can train your mind to find the good in people, you will find yourself naturally doing the same in all areas of your life.

"Keep your face to the sun and you will never see the shadows."

– HELEN KELLER

"Hope is sweet-minded and sweet-eyed. It draws pictures, it weaves fancies, it fills the future with delight."

– HENRY WARD BEECHER

LAUGH

Seek out something that will give you a good laugh every day and reap a whole range of psychological benefits. Whether it's through watching a favorite comedy show on TV or catching up with a funny friend, a good dose of laughter suddenly makes the future feel a whole lot brighter.

"If we were logical, the future would be bleak indeed. But we are more than logical. We are human beings, and we have faith, and we have hope."

– JACQUES COUSTEAU

"Hope is not a dream but a way of making dreams become reality."

– L.J. SUENENS

SET SMART GOALS

Having practical goals to work toward is an effective way to weave hope through your life. Make sure each of these goals is:

1. Specific

2. Measurable

3. Achievable

4. Relevant

5. Time-bound

"Believe in yourself and all that you are. Know that there is something inside you that is greater than any obstacle."

– CHRISTIAN D. LARSON

"Learn from yesterday, live for today, hope for tomorrow. The important thing is not to stop questioning."

– ALBERT EINSTEIN

"Sometimes good things fall apart so better things can fall together."

- MARILYN MONROE

BE PATIENT

Everyone has good days and bad days. Sometimes the bad days
just take a little time to sort out.

"Hope rises like a phoenix from the ashes of shattered dreams."

– S.A. SACHS

"For what it's worth…
it's never too late, or in
my case too early, to be
whoever you want to be."

– F. SCOTT FITZGERALD

JOURNAL

Make journaling a habit. Each week make a note of one good thing and one bad thing that has happened to you. Consider why you aren't entirely to blame for the bad event, and how the effects of it will soon pass. Find the lesson. Focus on the good event and consider how your actions impacted on this, how you can repeat it, or make the affects of it last.

"Rock bottom became
the solid foundation on
which I rebuilt my life."

– J.K. ROWLING

"Of all ills that one endures, hope is a cheap and universal cure."

– ABRAHAM COWLEY

EAT HEALTHILY

Looking after your body is an essential component in living a positive, hopeful life. It takes energy to have hope, so take good care of your body by feeding it healthy, balanced, and nutritious food that will support you from the inside.

"He who has health has hope; and he who has hope has everything."

— ARABIAN PROVERB

"Hope arouses, as nothing else can arouse, a passion for the possible."

– WILLIAM SLOANE COFFIN

KEEP POSITIVE COMPANY

Surround yourself with upbeat people who have a sense of purpose and passion and their attitude will rub off on you.

"Isn't it nice to think that tomorrow is a new day with no mistakes in it yet?"

– LUCY MAUD MONTGOMERY

"Hope means hoping when everything seems hopeless."

– G.K. CHESTERTON

IMMERSE YOURSELF IN ART

Find an artist or artwork you love and spend time viewing their work. If you can't make it to a gallery, simply browse online. Choose images you find full of hope and allow them to alter your perspective and mood, to motivate and inspire you.

"Even in the mud
and scum of things,
something always,
always sings."

– RALPH WALDO EMERSON

"All human wisdom
is summed up in two
words; wait and hope."

– ALEXANDRE DUMAS

SHARE WITH LOVED ONES

Share your deepest desires and dreams with the people you love and allow them to join you on your journey.

"If you lose hope, somehow you lose the vitality that keeps moving, you lose that courage to be, that quality that helps you go on in spite of it all. And so today I still have a dream."

– MARTIN LUTHER KING, JR.

"However bad life may seem, there is always something you can do and succeed at. Where there's life, there's hope."

– STEPHEN HAWKING

EVALUATE YOUR FEARS

Write down what it is you're afraid of and why. Once you identify and analyze your fears it's much easier to keep them in check.

"I know that you cannot live on hope alone, but without it, life is not worth living."

– HARVEY MILK

TAKE MINI-BREAKS

Take breaks of anything from 30 seconds through to a few minutes at least 3 times a day. Use this time, wherever you are, to shift your focus onto something that ignites positive feelings. For example, simply look away from your computer screen and focus on a tree outside, or the clouds drifting across the sky.

"Carve a tunnel of hope
through the dark mountain
of disappointment."

– MARTIN LUTHER KING, JR.

"Find the seed at the bottom of your heart and bring forth a flower."

– SHIGENORI KAMEOKA

RECONNECT WITH NATURE

Lift your spirits by spending time outside in nature. Take a walk through a forest, spend a night under the stars, or even just find a few moments to sit on a patch of grass in your garden.

"It is difficult to say what is impossible, for the dream of yesterday is the hope of today and the reality of tomorrow."

– ROBERT H. GODDARD

"If you wish to succeed in life, make perseverance your bosom friend, experience your wise counselor, caution your elder brother, and hope your guardian genius."

– JOSEPH ADDISON

"Keep a little fire burning; however small, however hidden."

– CORMAC MCCARTHY

MAKE A TO-TRY LIST

Nurture hope by making a list of interesting things you'd like to try, but haven't yet. Just setting the intention will give you things to look forward to, making you feel more hopeful about the future.

"In this life, anything can happen—and what can help bring it to pass is Hope."

– CLAUDE M. BRISTOL

"Hope cherishes no illusions, nor does it yield to cynicism."

— FATHER JAMES KELLER

"Hope sees the invisible, feels the intangible, and achieves the impossible."

– UNKNOWN

BECOME A ROLE MODEL

Become a role model for others by acting in a hopeful manner, regardless of your circumstances or mood. In the process of this active effort, as well as being a positive influence on others, you will actually become more hopeful yourself.

"Sometimes when you least expect it, the tables turn and that scary feeling that has taken hold of you for so long somehow turns into hope."

– DAVID ARCHULETA

"We must pass through the darkness, to reach the light."

– ALBERT PIKE

REFRAME YOUR SITUATION

It's all about interpretation of any given set of circumstances—
you can view something as disastrous and overwhelming, which
will inevitably lead to feelings of hopelessness, or as a lesson and
an opportunity to move forward in your life, which in contrast
will make you feel empowered and upbeat.

"What we call our despair is often only the painful eagerness of unfed hope."

– GEORGE ELIOT

PERFORM AN ACT OF KINDNESS

Performing random acts of kindness on a daily basis can dramatically impact on your mood and outlook. The smallest gestures can go a long way toward helping you to feel connected and as though you are making a worthwhile contribution to humanity.

"We live by hope. We do not always get all we want when we want it. But we have to believe that someday, somehow, some way, it will be better and that we can make it so."

– HUBERT H. HUMPHREY, JR.

"Man is a creature of hope and invention, both of which belie the idea that things cannot be changed."

– TOM CLANCY

BE COURAGEOUS

Cultivating hope requires courage to take that first step forward toward tackling your challenges. Be brave and begin.

"It's a lot better to hope than not to."

– BEN STEIN

"Hope...Sometimes that's all you have when you have nothing else. If you have it, you have everything."

– UNKNOWN

DON'T SWEAT THE SMALL STUFF

When we go through tough times, we adopt survival patterns to get us through. While these can be effective in times of turmoil, they are not suitable for everyday living, so we need to stop applying the same techniques to daily concerns and niggles. Remember that the vast majority of small stuff sorts itself out, so stop agonizing over it.

THIS TOO SHALL PASS

Remember that all suffering, all bad moments in time, will pass.

"The one law that does not change is that everything changes, and the hardship I was bearing today was only a breath away from the pleasures I would have tomorrow, and those pleasures would be all the richer because of the memories of this I was enduring."

– LOUIS L'AMOUR

"Hope, that star of life's
tremulous ocean."

– PAUL MOON JAMES

"Faith goes up the stairs that love has built and looks out the windows which hope has opened."

– CHARLES HADDON SPURGEON

FOCUS ON THE GOOD THINGS IN LIFE

Don't let all the bad things that are going on in the world overshadow the good. In every corner there is good to be found. Nurture a hopeful attitude by noticing the commonplace everyday kindnesses that are going on all around you.

"Hope is the last thing
ever lost."

– ITALIAN PROVERB

"I find hope in the darkest of days, and focus in the brightest. I do not judge the universe."

– DALAI LAMA

CREATE SPACE FOR HOPE

Let go of anything that is holding you back—your anxieties, worries, sadness, and self-doubt. Try to make space in your mind for hope.

"It's always something, to know you've done the most you could. But, don't leave off hoping, or it's of no use doing anything. Hope, hope to the last!"

– CHARLES DICKENS

"The wings of hope carry us, soaring high above the driving winds of life."

– ANA JACOB

LISTEN TO SOMEONE ELSE'S STORY

Make a point to ask an older friend or family member to tell you a meaningful story from their life. Seek to gain perspective and inspiration through their wisdom and experience.

"True hope dwells on the possible, even when life seems to be a plot written by someone who wants to see how much adversity we can overcome."

– WALTER ANDERSON

"Hope has as many lives as
a cat or a king."

– HENRY WADSWORTH LONGFELLOW

"While the heart beats,
hope lingers."

– ALISON CROGGON

DON'T TAKE LIFE TOO SERIOUSLY

Sometimes we can get so caught up in our pursuit of aspirations that we forget to enjoy the lighter aspects of life. Engage in a light-hearted activity today, just for the fun of it—the more "out of character" the better!

"A lesson for all of us is that for every loss, there is victory, for every sadness, there is joy, and when you think you've lost everything, there is hope."

– GERALDINE SOLON

"No winter lasts forever; no spring skips it's turn."

– HAL BORLAND